The Testimony of Witnesses

Kerry Tankard

The Testimony of Witnesses

Published by TSF, Peterborough

ISBN: 978-1-4716-6270-6

Cover photos taken by Kerry Tankard, 2011
Acknowledgment to www.Lulu.com for assistance

What follows is a series of poems written in response either to the story of Jesus, or to stories he told from the time he turned towards Jerusalem. The collection was originally written as a process of reflection in Lent, which is why the very first poem is written about Jesus' journey into the desert.

The collection can be read in any way that suits you. However, should you wish to use it as a Lenten journey then begin on Ash Wednesday, with *Face the City,* and follow each day from there.

CONTENTS

Watch for this Wasteland

Luke 4.1-13

Watch for this wasteland,
it will burn minds and
desecrate memories.
Here the wind cuts flesh
and sand draws the last drop of love from hearts.

Lips will break and words shatter on rocks;
stones in hands are opened and yeast,
the bacteria for life,
breeds a promise that beckons
but does not satisfy.

Glimpse from the heights
the lonely lands populated
by power that you could hold,
control.
Surrender your soul
to the balance sheet that shits
on lives discounted as commodities;
named worthless.

Fall in faith
forward
be a god among, only, men
be your own contempt
and forget why you ever came.

Watch for this wasteland. Watch. Watch and pray.

Face the City

Luke 9.51-56

Do you see the city?
Her towers rise piercing the sky;
Babel monoliths that still believe
in their own dominance.

In these streets there was welcome
and now resides the tinge of threat;
it is unspoken
but its caustic presence is the nausea
that plagues your stomach.

Shall you walk the line that leads,
or be lost in the land that surrounds;
Misdirected steps towards,
or run back to desert lands?

Feeble,
what are you against this panoply of power?
do you believe, for one moment, love can conquer here?

The City Sleeps?

Luke 9.57-62

Foxes have holes,
and birds their nests,
but the son of man has nowhere
to lay his head.

Fox, the city's wild walker, is resting,
hiding beneath the mounded earth,
she has fed;
feasted in the dark night
troubling the local livestock
with a distant furtive glance.

And above rests the slightness of chaffinch
who did not keep a nocturnal watch
over the passing and returning.
Instead she played the helpless sleeping soul
'til daylight carried her to seeds
for the night watch to pass again
without disturbance or dismay.

And yet in the city, sleeps
the man whose dreams were not disturbed
by passing steps.
Ignored by chaffinch and by fox,

over /

this stranger’s bed
left unperturbed by comfort,
became a holy icon
on which the holy would not look.

Poignant

Luke 10.1-4

Lambs into the midst of wolves
the ABC and RD
in conversation playing,

but who's the lamb
and who's the wolf
and who inhabits daydreams?

[The ABC is Rowan Williams and RD is Richard Dawkins and refers to a dialogue they had in March 2012]

Learning Humility

Luke 10.17-20

Do not presume what you can do
can undo what has been done.
But, the done can be undone
and new things yet become.

To the Trinity

Luke 10.21-24

See the three
in one entwining dance.
Each motion, step and stop,
each fleeting glance
captures the flush,
the confession of love,
disclosed by a subtle blush.

They embrace in a sudden still,
they fall, one,
bound in their even-song.
Held, they halt, breathe,
then move, not by chance.

Three divine movements
offer
their single performance.

Love You? Love Me?

Luke 10.25-28

I hold this delicate life.
I fear it will shatter
if held too tight or loose.

It lies in my hand;
I dare not breathe,
lest the least movement
would destroy
what I behold.

Do you bear me with such tenderness?

For I am what it is I fear;
I am the brittle so easily broken.
Can I love you,
before I learn to love me?

The Good Samaritan

Luke 29-37

Steps become quicker,
as the stench of sickly suffering
is dismissed by a thurible;

Overpowered by holiness,
dismissed by a wave;
as hands too busy praising, praying,
find no time to bend and tend.

What is bruised and broken
waits for a stranger,
who knows no better
than to see beyond the barrier;
kiss with compassion
these wounds that tell a tale.

I long for neither a seat in heaven
nor one in church,
but if you will notice my face
you'll see,
I see
with grace.

I did not choose

Luke 10.38-42

I did not choose this part;
I do not despise those who find the time
to sit
and wait
and listen
and learn
and be;
be loved
and held
by words,
by peace,
by grace,
by eyes,
eyes that promise hope
and undo all the hurt that's past.

But I did not choose this part; it chose me.

Do not teach me how to pray

Luke 11.1-4

My most primal cry
and yet not natural at all;
to stop still
and wait

on the silence of God

wondering if words
will break

the

pause

that stretches out
from the mouth of eternity.

A hand holds me here,
guides me as I do not see:
not blinded by holiness,
but lost in the dance
of love:
that is the love-to-love-to-love
that loves me.

Knock and Ask

Luke 11.5-13

Up in the night in the darkness I stumble;
with sound, not sight, I audibly grumble.
Disturbing the livestock, the kids and the wife
because my neighbour's in some bloody strife.

Disturbed in the darkness to answer distress;
he's asking for bread, and I'm not even dressed.
All I wanted was silence, and sleep to enhance,
my dreams, where so strangely, I find I can dance!

But here, hardly dressed, in the doorway I stand
with a quizzical look and a loaf in my hand.
Now tell me God, as I'm calm at the door,
would you be so calm if I woke you at four?

The Sign of the Carbon Divine

Luke 11.29-32

Carbon sign;
the Divine vein,
becomes the line
that writes the word
that becomes flesh
that is the sign
that leads to
leads to
leads

readers to a possibility
posited in their midst;
that what they seek
is not afar
but in the space
that makes sense
of words
walking the line
of the Carbon Divine.

Fear?

Luke 12.4-7

I hear,
but I do not fear,
not if by fear
I'm meant to tremble,
quake in the face of the One
who considers
sparrows.

What I see
when I hear
of fear, is surprise,
that the one who could kill,
who could banish,
has stilled
and counted:
counted my hairs

So, do I fear?
Or, do I be not afraid?

Acknowledgement

Luke 12.8-12

Who is She,
whose whispered words
unveil a face
that looks
beyond the pallor
to see the reddening heart?

Guilt beneath the gilt on flesh;
the troubled mind is restless:
longing to be possessed
not overpowered.

So it is
the unacknowledged
falls forward to hope
in
She Who Is, Who She Is.

Hesed

Luke 12.13-21

I do not hold back my generous hand:
I pour from it, in the yield of the land.
But did you consider, sipping your wine,
what it was you enjoyed, and why I cried?

This love was breaking the boundaries set
so you tore them down, no sense of regret.
But stood with pride over all you'd received;
never a question of how you deceived

yourself to believe that all this was yours.
No prompt in your heart that this love abhors
self-satisfaction that simply excludes
the voice that still speaks in beatitudes.

Lily

Luke 12.22-31

She rises in the emerald landscape.
A delicate strength, set apart
by an austerity of chiffon petals
that gently bow to draw the eye.

In her regarded beauty,
where nature paints more perfectly,
there is calm and comfort
as worry fades before life.

Her strength and simplicity
invite a memory
that will allay anxiety
as her perfume breathes a stillness over all.

Purses

Luke 12.32-34

Purses in heaven
not worn out by endless use
nor are they stolen

Anticipation

Luke 12.35-40

Gowns flow like oil,
spilling onto the ground;
there is enough to waste.

This is celebration born
from perpetual anticipation,
as the waiting become the waited on.

The descent of *Oikonomos*

Luke 12.41-48

Empowered for economy
not limited to a house,
this is the descent of oikonomos
and why the judgement's right.

The servants of a master
whose name was never God,
instead it's the filthy lucre
Jonny Rotten spoke about.

They stand in a middle
occupying unhallowed ground,
but who's questioning the motives
embraced by senior clowns.

Let the countries falter,
and let the hungry starve,
so long as the hedge fund's master,
just submit to capital's crown.

Kindling and Kin

Luke 12.49-53

The kindling sparks
craving to become fire

Burn
Enflame
disrupt in waves
and distort vision

What do we say now of divided kin?

Before and After

Luke 13.10-17

Before

stumbling steps defined me
in other people's eyes.

After

I gazed into eyes
as for the first time;
seeing and being seen.

The Yeast that Leavens

Luke 13.18-21

See the subtle movement

signs of life in the once inanimate

the breathing presence
a Spirit's disturbance

the yeast
that leavens the batch

so the hungry feed
on that which was not fit
for Passover

At Your Door

Luke 13.22-30

I know those eyes
the creeping story telling lines
echoes of laughter and tears
long since passed away

they have dwelt
on my darkest days,
seen the soul secreted safely
out of the sight of strangers

so I fall at your door

inside there stands the table,
the host of all our tales,
the meal time celebrations
the stains of spilt ales

the crumbs of bread, broken,
captured in the creases of my clothes,
each fragment a sacred statement
that all is not lost

so I fall at your door

?

Luke 14.1-6

The Rabbi’s question
invokes a sudden silence.
Judgement? Forgiven.

Take a Seat

Luke 14.7-11

The priest takes his seat
before the bride and groom;
believing his importance
he displaces all the room.

As warning looks question
his overblown self-perception
and the immanent descension
that will expose him as a fool.

The full bodied wine of laughter
will follow him even after
he has reddened like the Rioja
he still clutches in his hand.

Escorted to the fringes,
re-seated so he listens
to the wisdom of the margins
as they offer simple pardons

that renew him by the presence
he dismissed with condescendence.
Take a seat, then wait to see
where you're moved.

Invitation

Luke 14.12-14

This invitation is not cast aside;
is not one more of many to be chosen between.
This is the only one;
the only one that ever mattered.
Now it has been opened is there is no saying no.

The guests gather
surviving the surprise of invitation,
the embossed letters declaring
welcome.
They chatter.
Their stuttering syllables proffer disbelief
that cannot revoke God's supplication.

Cost

Luke 14.25-33

Weigh up this moment
and dare to anticipate
at what cost this comes.

When love is balanced
against all you will let go,
what is it you hold?

home away home

Luke 15.11-19

Home was where I'd suffocated
felt controlled by complicated
boundaries that govern
all the freedom for which I'd longed.

Away is where I found myself
dismembered disremembered
first controlling then disowning
who I was failing to become.

So home is where I longed for
not forgotten and not undone
but a waiting place where I knew
once again I'd just belong.

Waiting

Luke 15.20-24

How long have I watched and plagued the landscape
with my search for signs;
waited to witness steps, even if they shudder in anxiety
or falter far from me?

How long have I anticipated the run and embrace
that retraces mistakes
until they no longer mark departure
but are erased by the boundary around return?

How long have I cried and wondered
why I cannot reach my loved one,
why he's hidden in a story I cannot read;
where secret pages turn, each one veiling pain.

Too long I have watched, waited and cried,
so I run without consideration
embrace with tears, whose heat will not scald,
as my heart burns in their release.

My father's other son

Luke 15.25-32

Bleeding hearts and liberals gather
round my father's hearth
but bitterness is tearing
my life,
my soul
apart.

I have worked
earned
given
done
for what,
as it's undone
by my father's other son,
by my father's other son.

Trust

Luke 16.10-13

She is the mystery who walks
in the sun
nothing hidden,
naked and unveiled.

Her unconcealed beauty
risks all
in the simple assurance
that what is done
has reason.

She follows in secret
lines walked in public;
no contradiction,
simply consistent,

the immanent
the economic
one.

The rich man and Lazarus

Luke16.19-31

warning words,
admonishing addresses

unheard

simply disregarded

comfort cushions
complacency lessens
concern for the invisible
locked out;
kept beyond the gate.

do the dogs mock
or weep with compassion
on the wounds of the neglected?

Forgiveness

Luke 17.1-4

Practise forgiveness.
Flavoured so bitter and sweet,
what does your mouth taste?

Gratitude

Luke 17.11-19

Gratitude

that effusion of enthusiasm
flowing fountain-like from hearts
and lives

looking to articulate
the moments that incarnate

salvation

a realized redemption

not in profound
but simple exchanges
of gracious consideration.

Thank you.

The flowering kingdom

Luke 17.20-25

A blossoming presence,
yet its subtle tones
could be almost lost
upon the landscape of desires.

It is a passion that flowers;
whose fragrance carries
to enchant those
who seek its meek aroma.

This vivid capacity to attract
does not possess, or luridly lure,
but teases with a playfulness
that respects the difference.

Not a thiefdom, but a kingdom
where Good shares herself with all;
she overflows, her love endows
the greatness in the small.

Righteous awakening

Luke 18.9-14

You dare to stand with
self-righteous indignation;
look down you smug fool.

Welcome the Children

Luke 18.15-17

Gone is the simplicity
where the rabbi welcomes
and the priest embraces
without discomfort.

People presume,
far beyond what is real,
in the action of an innocent
who simply remains
to ensure the neglected
are not misdirected
by rejection.

Hold them
while you forgive a world
its false presumption.
Agape lives on.

Impossible

Luke 18.18-27

I see the impossible as earth is broken
by that which was presumed dead, hidden.

I consume the impossible as bread is broken, wine poured;
tasting heaven in her disguised Lord.

I hear the impossible as She breathes her love:
the one who beholds me tells me I'm beautiful.

I am not the impossible
but I know who is,
despite the objections.

Follow

Luke 18.28-34

Begin to follow

But be careful with your steps

Choose each one wisely.

The Misunderstood

Luke 19.1-10

Judged in whispered voices
that gather and presume
they know more about me
than they're really free to assume.

I walk the line of compromise
in court rooms, on trading floors,
trying to practise justice
isn't easy, but I'm sure

that you've never understood,
with your prejudice proclaimed first,
what it means to trade fairly,
help the arrested ease their thirst.

You can pray for all vocations
and leave mine sat outside,
as I practise a hidden benevolence
so readily denied.

As the holy huddles gather
who never walked my line,
I'm another climbing Zacchaeus
whom Jesus recognized in time.

Silence and Stones

Luke 19.29-40

Can the stones cry out
if people are silenced,
or will they be lifted
and thrown,
a violence
reminding God,
should she need it,
that he who passes by
will walk these streets,
and die.

The Last Week

Luke 19.45-48

Words of wisdom fall
at feet that kick them away.
So the end arrives.

Gift

Luke 20.45-21.4

It leaves your hand

weightless

floating.

Its lightness has no depth
a colourless contribution
changing nothing

passing one to an other

this is no gift.

Yet a gift is given
whose burden of weight,
to the one who lets go,
goes unnoticed
by the passing crowd

This unbearable lightness
only God can carry.

Judas

Luke 21.37-22.3

Semblant disciple?
Take your tortured turn,
while denying past and present,
weary of hope that has not flourished in time.

What broken desire is it
that goes unfilled in a veiled torment?
A portent of the end that is arriving.

Who failed in this falling?
Was it better not to be born
as faith fractured and the heart tore?

Remember

Luke 22.39-46

The poet remembers
paints
portrays
blossoming beads
sweat that bleeds
in salted pearls of desperation
seasoning earth's anticipation.

Here the cup does not run over
with anything more
than soured wine.
Remember?

Fervent silence
the only sound
that breaks the night
before the shouts,
the kiss.

The friends now fled.

This anamnesis will awaken
those who sleep at the dawn
of death's sunset.

Golgotha

Luke 23.32-38

Golgotha
mound for the mauling of life
crowned in crosses and jewelled by bodies
this skull has lost its mind.

The dark sockets
recesses that no longer see
in the darkest daylight.

Holy Saturday

Luke 23.50-56

Laid still in silence
sweet spices anoint the corpse
death denies all hope

The Testimony of Witnesses

Luke 24.1-12

Hear my idle tale.
I do not care about your disbelief,
test it if you must,
but know his body is not claimed by dust.

Here there is emptiness
that is not bleak despairing.
Instead hear the whispers of angels
who defy reason
and shake the foundations
that once made you secure
like the door that sealed the dead.

The unmovable is displaced,
as the sand is imprinted with studded footprints.

www.ingramcontent.com/pod-product-compliance
Ingram Content Group UK Ltd.
Pitfield, Milton Keynes, MK11 3LW, UK
UKHW020232250726
13967UKWH00001B/317